Dr. Gunjeet Kaur-Profile:

A Ph. D in Marketing with three decades plus of experience as a CRM, Brand and Image Consultant & Trainer to several multi-national, public sector and small companies, she is also a reputed Speaker at Brand Image Seminars and has been recognized by Indian Ministry of Commerce for contribution to industry. Owner of several copyrights & a Patent (filed), throughout her career she has held senior positions, worked with every strata of management from CEOs to young executives, freelancers to students of both genders.

Recreational Cannabis and Canada- Look Who's Dancing© !!

Federal Government of Canada legalized recreational cannabis in 2018 after which it started a movement towards a tightly regulated private retail model for cannabis by opening 4 provinces immediately to private sector retailers with plans of opening others by April 2019. (https://www.ontario.ca/page/cannabis-legalization). In 2019, the total sales from cannabis market in Canada (including medical, illegal, and legal recreational products) are expected to be up to $7.17 billion. Statistics Canada estimates that 5.4 million people are expected to want to buy legal cannabis in the fourth quarter of 2018 and 1.7 million people will continue to buy illegal cannabis (https://www150.statcan.gc.ca/n1/daily-quotidien/181017/dq181017c-eng.htm accessed 14 nov '18)

Cannabis, also known as grass, pot or marijuana, has spurred abundant controversy over the past century. For a long time, people have utilized cannabis as drug or for psychedelic trips. In Canada, its been illegal since it started- that, however, didn't suit the Canadians who wanted to dance to the tune of legalized fun. At that point, people proposed and Govt of Canada took action accordingly.

Cannabis, also known as grass, pot or marijuana, has spurred abundant controversy over the past century. With an annual consumption by an estimated 160 million people (4% of the world's population), cannabis is estimated to be the world's third most popular recreational drug after alcohol and tobacco,. With **cannabis recreational legalization** spreading throughout the country, priority of recreational marketers is to shift the perception of the market and public about cannabis users from "stoner" stereotypes to a mix of white-collar executives and older generation.

Trying to build a house without engineering measures or an architecture plan doesn't work- sales of legalized cannabis and making people dance to its tune requires segmentation of recreational users in Canada. Marketers are actively seeking indicators for the development of recreational use products and associated positioning to develop a relationship with this new market in which relationship can have a much longer life cycle leading to higher ROI due to the popularity of the product.

To identify such target market, many firms start with the differences based on demography or on other psychographic factors but, as opined by Forsyth et al (1999) firms find that consumer demographics or psychographics alone do not give a complete picture of consumer behavior as all baby boomers do not have the same preferences, all young women between the ages of 18 and 24 do not display same patterns of behavior, and geo demographic classifications do not justify the reason why people in one street drive different cars, read different newspapers, eat different food and so on.

Similarly, due to an assumption of profits being dependent on customers inherent in the Profitability Segmentation Model, it is flawed as profits are a function of processes and offerings that a firm uses to fulfill customer needs and usage preferences that lead to customer satisfaction. "The customer does not know which chair he wants unless he sees it" (Freytag & Nielsen, 1990)

Segmentation strategies enabling marketers to define segments in a specific measurable manner that is meaningful to ROI are rare. This book attempts to fill this void in the literature by profiling post-legalization likely Recreational Cannabis User in Canada on tangible "purpose" basis thus creating an "actionable segmentation". It becomes easier to act on this basis as measurable segments can be more easily translated into profitability and ROI, strategic and tactical marketing imperatives, specific channel delivery systems and stronger relationships.. This weeds out the guesswork involved in translating "psychographic" segments and profiles.

"Purpose" in this ,

a. is considered different from the reason in the sense that purpose is the "tangible end goal" (what is the product for?) whereas reason is a "psychological guess"(why do you want it?) usually based on traditional segmentation variables of age, income, stage in the family life cycle and social class. Harrison (1994) concludes that "these variables have provided little insight into the customer behavior" thereby validating that reason is a guess-basis of segmentation. The differences in perceptions are due to the different purposes for which every customer uses the product- thus

seeking a "fit" through purpose satisfying product
attributes.

b. is considered different from the traditional
definition of "needs and want or benefits" as these
focus on the hidden motivations of the customer or
economic/lifestyle symbolisms

The structure of the book is organized to start with a
discussion on the role of segmentation in enhancing
customer focus and relationships with a goal of enabling
customization with validations from the previous research
on segmentation. Next section discusses the research
methodology detailing the survey modality, sample size,
and statistical tools used for interpretation and analysis. An
analysis of results and findings follow describing the
importance of factors to current and likely users of
legalized recreational cannabis and developing a correlation
between variables to provide a meaningful segmentation.
Next, the book develops a Specific Profiling of the likely

cannabis users post-legalization in Canada. The specificity

of profiling is focused on making the segment "actionable",

measurable, and customization friendly.

SEGMENTATION- A SALES PROGRAM IN DISGUISE

Market segmentation should be the core of strategic decision-making through data analysis techniques and new basis of segmentation. If this focus was done properly, it will maximize returns for a given marketing expenditure. An analysis of successful firms in B2C and B2B markets as measured by reduction in customer acquisition cost, increase ion customer response, and less chances of product failure validates the role of effective ROI enhancing segmentation strategy. Segmentation is a tool with power to enable a value based ranking of customers for better ROI based investment decisions with inherent potential to drive business growth

The need to challenge our mental models of segmentation becomes necessary with the changing business environment, implications of operating in a global information age, the rise of empowered consumers and

9

digital networks The preferences as predetermined by a customer are based on the purpose for which he is buying a product and it is this purpose that decides his level of post-consumption satisfaction as fulfillment of a purpose is the most observable and measurable indicator. In fact, it is this basis of purpose where the *perception* of "product fulfilling its promise" and *actual* fulfillment are one and the same thing- perception becomes measurable objectively. .For example, cannabis users typically buy dope to "experience something" that is totally measurable as it is a "state/feel of their mind". (stress reliever, pain relief, psychedelic experience, etc). (https://www150.statcan.gc.ca/n1/daily-quotidien/180718/dq180718b-eng.htm)

In other words, the differences in perceptions are due to the different purposes for which every customer uses the product- thus seeking a "fit" through purpose satisfying product attributes. One of the main ways of serving customer is through customized communication of goal satisfying attributes of product offering- a communication based on an understanding of the "customer's buying purpose" . A purpose based segmentation is aimed at a more efficient use of marketing resources by customizing messages, offers, and customer relationship management initiatives to customers who will be most responsive in the chosen segments as they see/feel an achievement of their tangible end goal. This becomes possible as the "fit" based on tangible "purpose" and the offering can be more easily demonstrated.

METHODOLOGY

The research study was empirical in nature with a questionnaires sent via email across all provinces of Canada. The basis of sample chosen to send these questionnaires was kept same as used by Government of Canada to survey tobacco and/or drug use monitoring and addiction with exclusion of territories, people without internet access, residents of institutions, homeless, and/or those unable to understand English or French.(https://www150.statcan.gc.ca/n1/pub/82-003-x/2018002/article/54908/tbl/ttbl01-eng.htm). The first level of population consisted of friends, relatives and other personal contacts of the author who were informed about the survey purpose, clauses of confidentiality, and who agreed to forward it to their network of 18 years of age and above residents.

As size of the sample is a one of the important determinants in measuring validity of the research, as first stage, 3768 emails(not including the bounced mails) were sent to Canadian residents detailing the nature of the survey, their right to refusal statement and seeking consent and permission to e-mail questionnaire. No incentive was provided for participation in the study. 2746 consent emails came back. In second stage of survey, questionnaires were e-mailed to these consenting respondents who were given 10 days timeline to revert with completed questionnaire. On receipt by researcher, 2120 were found to be usable and were used to calculate results and findings.

The questionnaire was divided into two sections-in the first section, questionnaire consisted of personal details of the selected customers as a voluntary option with inherent confidentiality clause. The second section consisted of questions related to various factors this paper sought to measure to segment the recreational cannabis market in Canada.

A multiple choice questionnaire was designed based on validated research (references 3-8).

Descriptive and inferential statistics were used to analyze the data. Average means scores of each factor were calculated. Pearson's coefficient of correlation was used to draw statistical inferences among various factors in order to get a more specific indication of segmentation.

RESULTS AND FINDINGS

The study revealed far-reaching insights on customers' purpose of usage and other factors of significant interest to a marketer in the new recreational cannabis use market in Canada.

An interesting finding was that the recreational users' viewed themselves as different from habitual users because they sought drug for a specific "beneficial" purpose as opposed to "addictive, psychedelic or other harmful" reasons. In addition, they considered the risks to be manageable.

Buying Frequency: Pre- & Post-Legalization

Table 1: Difference in Buying Frequency Pre- & Post Legalization(Current & Likely Buyers)

Frequent users	+23.49%
Less frequent users	+183%

A substantial number of *Post-legalization likely users in the less frequent users* led to a positive 183% increase in buying frequency. This new segment of likely users is non-habitual though have consumed cannabis sometimes in their life and have full control over how much and when they consume. These use cannabis products infrequently (averaging to once in 1.27 months)

Factors Impacting Buying Decision Post-Legalization

Table 2: Factors Impacting Buying Decision Post-Legalization

Factor	Importance	Difference Between Current & Likely Users
Reasonable price	High	Less important to likely than current users(-12%)
Reputation of Grower	High	More important to likely than current users(+29%)

Better Quality of Products	High	More important to likely than current users (+32%)
Type of cannabis product	Medium	Less important to likely than current users(-16%)
Tried by me before	Low	Less important to likely than current users (-8%)
Familiar brand		No significant difference
Preferred Potency Available	Low	Less important to likely than current users(-23%)
Anti- Pesticide tested	Low	No significant difference
Others	Low	No significant difference

Reasonable price, grower reputation, and better quality of products were the top three most important factors impacting buying decision of both current and likely buyers of recreational cannabis out of which reputation of the grower showed significant increase in the importance to likely buyers. Familiarity of brand and tried product as factors were not preferred by significant percentage of respondents to be considered as important factors.

Reasonable price ranged between $8-15 with the new likely users post legalization showing price insensitivity.

Purpose of Recreational Cannabis Usage

Table 3: Purpose of Recreational Cannabis Use By Importance

Purpose of Recreational Cannabis Use	%age of Buyers
Social Bonding with Friends	75
As Stress Reliever	74
Alcohol Replacement/Complement	69

As Mood Lifter	43
Sexual Performance Enhancer	21
For Sensory Uplift	18
Others	8

Relieving stress, supporting partying and fun with friends, and replacing alcohol were the top three purposes of buying recreational cannabis amongst both current and likely users pre-and post-legalization in Canada. The result clearly indicates an emphasis on tangible and measurable outcomes of cannabis consumption as opposed to subjective perceptual "needs" of "psychedelic experiences".

Factors Impacting Format of Purchase- Physical Store vs E-Store

Given the fact that likely users segment is more educated than current users (with minimum under-graduate degree), it was no surprise that clarity of details about pricing was a top factor to the likely users. It was of importance to current users also though the main reason was that current users were price elastic whereas likely users wanted transparency. This was found to be of no. 1 importance in both formats of sale. Grower details were a factor of high importance to likely users as compared to current users and payment options were high in importance to current users who wanted a variety of payment options.

Table 4: Importance of Factors in Physical vs Online Store

Factor	Difference between Current & Likely Users	Importance of Factor	Format(Physical Store vs E-Store)
4.1 Clearly marked prices for all products	More important to likely	High	Both

	than current users(+29%)		
4.2 Grower details	More important to likely than current users(+46%)	High	Both
4.3 Privacy protection and cybersecurity	No significant difference	High	Both
4.4 Sales Rep's Knowledge of Product	No significant difference	Low	Both

4.5 Polite Behaviour of Sales Reps	No significant difference	High	E-Store
4.6 Payment options	Less important to likely than current users(-32%)	Low	Both
4.7 Free Shipping	No significant difference	High	E-Store
4.8 Ease of searching/finding products	No significant difference	High	Physical Store
4.9 Variety of Products	No significant	High	Both

difference

4.10 Timing of Store	No significant difference	Low	Physical Store

Reputation of grower came out as a significant factor especially to likely users who will buy post-legalization recreational cannabis. Analysis revealed a strong co-relation between the reputation of grower and level of price (although likely users showed price inelasticity) and quality of products. In fact, as indicated by the table, the 2nd most important purpose of usage, recreational cannabis as a stress reliever, had a significant correlation with the reputation of grower thereby indicating that users, in particular the likely users, connect the grower's image directly with whether the product will fulfill the purpose for which they are buying it.

Further, grower details displayed a significantly high correlation with quality of product indicating that users considered the product to be of a high quality if it had constituents from a reputed grower of cannabis. These findings about growers have important implications for Policy makers as the growers in Canada are licensed by the Federal Government.

As an indicator of preferences in buying channels, there was no major difference in choices of physical vs online format of sale. Sales representatives'/customer service representatives' knowledge about the recreational cannabis product had significantly high correlation when the purpose of buying was as an alcohol replacement/supplement. This indicates that buyers consider recreational cannabis in the same category as alcohol and will prefer someone to tell them about the quality and constitution details of this new product just like they want the same details when they buy

alcohol.

ACTIONABLE SEGMENTATION- PROFILING CANADA' POST-LEGALIZATION PURPOSIVE RECREATIONAL CANNABIS USERS

"Actionable Segmentation" is an outcome of Canada's Post-Legalization Recreational Cannabis Users showing a new segment emerged due to the legalization. The survey results allowed a 'Specific Profiling' of these users to ensure that this segment becomes more measurable and concretized to enable the Strategy makers and marketers to focus their ROI plans by integrating customized processes and offerings. Customization, the core of customer relationship marketing, is the basis of greater value creation through differentiation leading to loyalty, profitability and long term return on their investment. Kaur (2016) stated that superior value creation is a result of two important processes of CRM- proactive customer business development and partnering relationships with lifetime value customers.

Cost reduction is made possible through this actionable segmentation as the new segment is clearly defined in tangible terms doing away with any requirement of irrelevant mass focused marketing tactics. Revenue generation becomes easier as the new segment is based on price, usage patterns, channel variable preferences, and most important purposes of using recreational cannabis. This actionable new emerging segment is spread across all provinces in Canada. Given the Per Capita Consumption of Cannabis in provinces and the per capita dollar value, this segment, that's price inelastic, has potential of generating a high ROI for marketing companies and retailers.

Table 6: Consumption of Cannabis Per Capita

	grams
Newfoundland and Labrador	18.52
Prince Edward Island	18.95
Nova Scotia	27.06
New Brunswick	20.46
Quebec	18.49
Ontario	21.00
Manitoba	18.31
Saskatchewan	16.37
Alberta	24.08
British Columbia	24.60

Table 6: Consumption of Cannabis Per Capita

	grams
Yukon	17.70
Northwest Territories	15.30
Nunavut	13.62

Source(s): Statistics Canada, National Gross Domestic Product by Income and by Expenditure Accounts (IEA) survey no. 1901. (https://www150.statcan.gc.ca/n1/daily-quotidien/180430/cg-b001-eng.htm)

Pre-legalization cannabis users were younger who experimented with all "pleasures of life" due to peer-group directions and "trend". The study reveals a new segment of likely users- aged between 36-57- majority of whom (82%) have used drugs sometimes in their life. Legalization has made this segment ready to try drugs again though these will be "infrequent users"- with frequency of usage ranging from once in 1.27 months.

This segment is a mix of males and females in almost equal number both with minimum college undergraduate degree. With family responsibilities, these will buy mainly to relieve stress and are aware of products available in the USA market. Overall control over drug habit is high with complete awareness of side effects beyond a particular potency/amount.

This is clearly different from current users who are younger (16-30), experimenters, majority lacking higher education, peer-group run, and are price sensitive. This new likely recreational segment further shows preference for eating rather than smoking cannabis. As they are socializers, they are more dependent on word-of-mouth as main source of information about drugs. Being aware of current affairs, they regularly follow Newspapers and know about changes in Government policies and other economy related events.

Fig 1: A Snapshot of Canada' Post-Legalization Likely Recreational Cannabis Users

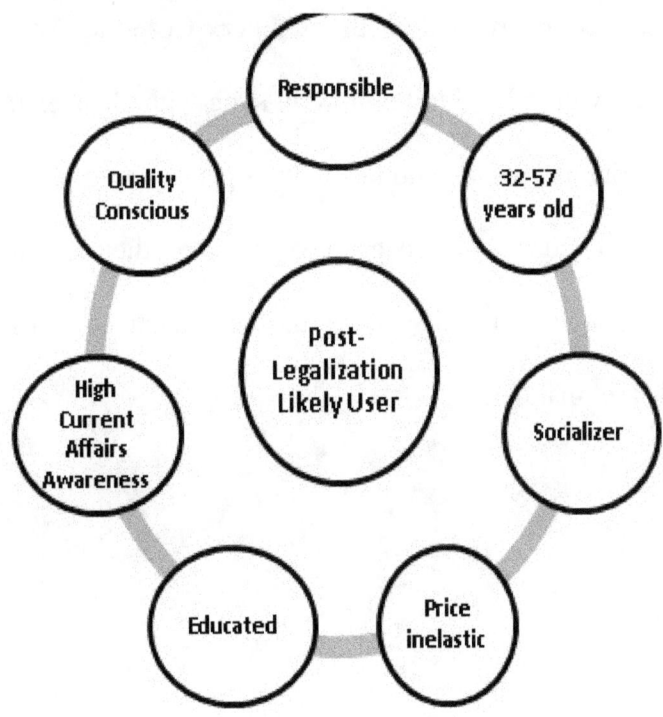

This clearly indicates an importance of marketing strategy centered on public relations, social networking, and positive word-of-mouth. As this segment is an aware segment that is educated, 'blind' and 'in-the-air' marketing tactics with non-validated content may harm the reputation of the company and/or the retailer. Corporate strategy makers would have to be more in sync with changes in the economy as a whole and keep eyes open for an opportunity developed due to these changes to tailor their marketing plan around so that it reaches the new segment in a more educated manner.

REFERENCES

Freytag, Per Vagn and Hobjerg, Ann Clark (2001). Business to Business Market Segmentation. *Industrial Marketing Management*, 30, 473-486.

Health Reports: Prevalence and correlates of non-medical only and self-defined medical and non-medical cannabis use,https://www150.statcan.gc.ca/n1/daily quotidien/180718/dq180718b-eng.htm,

---

Legalization of Cannabis in Canada https://www.ontario.ca/page/cannabis-legalization,

Survey Design Information. https://www150.statcan.gc.ca/n1/pub/82-003-x/2018002/article/54908/tbl/ttbl01-eng.htm

Value Added. https://www150.statcan.gc.ca/n1/daily-quotidien/180430/dq180430b-eng.htm